LIBRARY OF SMALL CA

LIBRARY OF SMALL CATASTROPHES

ALISON C. ROLLINS

COPPER CANYON PRESS
PORT TOWNSEND, WASHINGTON

Cover art: Nick Cave, *Soundsuit*, 2008. Mixed media. Copyright Nick Cave.
Photo by James Prinz Photography. Courtesy of the artist and Jack Shainman
Gallery, New York.

Copper Canyon Press is in residence at Fort Worden State Park in Port
Townsend, Washington, under the auspices of Centrum. Centrum is a
gathering place for artists and creative thinkers from around the world,
students of all ages and backgrounds, and audiences seeking extraordinary
cultural enrichment.

LIBRARY OF CONGRESS CATALOGING-IN-PUBLICATION DATA
Names: Rollins, Alison C., author.
Title: Library of small catastrophes / Alison C. Rollins.
Description: Port Townsend, Washington : Copper Canyon Press, [2019]
Identifiers: LCCN 2018039373 | ISBN 9781556595394 (pbk. : alk. paper)
Classification: LCC PS3618.O549 A6 2019 | DDC 811/.6—dc23
LC record available at https://lccn.loc.gov/2018039373

9 8 7 6 5 4 3 2 first printing

Copper Canyon Press
Post Office Box 271
Port Townsend, Washington 98368
www.coppercanyonpress.org

Nothin' is for sure
Nothin' is for certain
Nothin' lasts forever

OutKast, "Aquemini"

I know now that what is tragic isn't the moment.
It is the memory.

Jacqueline Woodson, *Another Brooklyn*

CONTENTS

I

II

III

LIBRARY OF SMALL CATASTROPHES

I

A Woman of Means

Venus Hottentot in a convex mirror
an interior coagulation of disembodiment.

They say that men are more visual & it is true
I can't see myself from behind.

Can't curate the archives of these cave-wall paintings
drawn with moist fingers and firm hands.

Today a man in a white coat told me
about my insides, read me my body aloud:

Is you is or is you ain't
my uterus in translation.

The language of anatomy
inextricably linked to word choice.

The autopsy made me aware of the leg-
less beast wriggling beneath my skin.

Violent sounds of silent gargling, the hot
throb of a breath pulsing the cold air.

You—the fox and the hound, the hunter
who pulls the trigger with his tongue.

Wet and bloody at the opening
silver claws and cotton teeth.

Pink goosebumps waddle the lips
a small vice, peculiar and wild.

Part my fur to the side.
Spirit says I am wolf.

Spirit tells me my blouse is damp with milk.
The white mystery of doubt now leaks.

I give you permission to enter—
the opulence of this rabbit hole.

Skinning Ghosts Alive

In the beginning, there is no yes.
The amniotic sac a dust jacket

for the book of trauma. One plus one makes one.
There is a nomenclature to this math, a method

to the madness of creation. There is no he.
There is no she. There's just a girl expelling

Y from her loose-jowled maw. The residue of jargon
stains her lips boy-red. We are never our own.

This is why we are so lonely. Why light-headed stars
nestle their knives in the sky's black chest. Why we

eat men like air. Moon's bulb shaved down to a hang-
nail's comma. Straight as the line that reads you

your missing period and the knowing that this cannot
be allowed to continue. This belly not permitted

to raise a question. Even lightning shakes the earth
like a daughter. Who am I to object? Point fingers at the order.

I was born bad. A train of *yeses* parading round
my hip's border. A trail of forget-me-nots sprouting
from my father's chin. This tongue needs shepherding,
as do these bones. I clench and carry the pain of my mother
in my teeth, at the root a canal of fear. The space between
each molar the size of the closet my grandmother's
mother locked her in as she cried *no* promising that she
would be good. So naturally my mouth's second nature is
naughty. This is how you end up leading the shell of a man
to your bed. How you crack your peanut-colored self

until the sidewalks of your cheeks are caked with salt.
Your lover's eyelids half-lit houses—terror veins its way
down the stairs. It is cold in this thing we call a body.
Who will tend to the fire with so few hands to go around?

Even a snake loses itself in its skin.
Its life's throat peeled back in molting song.

A second me lies somewhere on the ground.
Hollowed as the cicada shells I collected in the woods

as a child. Knowing then that the anatomy of loss
was worth picking, if only to acknowledge that

something has shed and not died, something brown as me
has left its skeleton behind, more intact than broken,

as if to say we are living
and dying just the same.

This is why we are so homesick,
why we hull ourselves in shadows.

original [sin]

In ancient Greece, for all her heroes, for Medea…
water meant death.

Jesmyn Ward, *Salvage the Bones*

i poured a bowl of cereal,
threw the empty box in the
trash can. grandaddy pulled

the box from the trash,
poured the crumbs into a
bowl, then doused the sand

in milk. he looked down at the
bowl, murmuring about how
he had survived the depression. told

a story about asking for hot water
at colored diners, how he would
pour ketchup in cups to make soup.

this was how
i first learned i am
wasteful.

* * *

i would stand in the bathroom
with my mother. would ask her
why the water in the bowl was

red. she would tell me she
had eaten beets. i suppose
i was too young to learn

the truth, milkflowers
spill petals red.

* * *

in my catholic school,
we took a beautifully wrapped box,
passed it around the class,

unwrapping it piece by piece.
afterward the teacher cleverly
explained that the box was

a girl's virginity

the gift we give our husbands.

& who wants a toy that has
already been opened? half
the joy is in untying the string.

this is how i was taught
that at my very core, i am
ungrateful.

* * *

maybe this is how i end up
throwing good things away:
phd
husband
stepdaughter
stepson

a little tiny baby
        unborn

locked them all in flooding
house with tearful grin.

this is how you
come to know you are
unclean.

          * * *

at times i smell of rain,
blouse damp with
a cloud of breast milk,

this stomach a
sloshing bowl of
watery swish.

i curse the phantom belly-
moon, can still hear the
sound of you in still water.

                 the wind begins to push
a heavy rain, drops spill from
every crevice of the flower.

pouring, the rain always all ways
asks for forgiveness.

a ghost kneels in me,
        asks to be spared.

mis·ery *n.* **1a.** A state of great unhappiness and emotional distress; **b.** as in, among the blacks is *misery* enough, God knows, but no poetry; **c.** speak of the devil; **d.** as in, among the off-color is a joke; **e.** as in, I no longer have my wits about me. **2a.** A cause or source of suffering; **b.** as in, *misery* loves company; **c.** as in, a sit-in; **d.** a gang of green; **e.** a coup d'etat of cells; **f.** the chicken or the egg; **g.** what the blood gets wind of; **h.** a necklace of braided rope; **i.** writing with a gun to the head; **j.** a body blow of dandy lions; **k.** as in, breaking silence by hand; **l.** the era of post-truth; **m.** the rain dragging its leg; **n.** as in, wailing blacks and blues; **o.** as in, have you no mercy?; **p.** to put it out of its *misery.*

The Fultz Quadruplets

*I knew God was a man because he put a baby in Mary
without her permission.*

Tyree Daye

The God is a white man.
The white man is a doctor.
The doctor is the one who
names things.

The doctor excitedly paces
the colored wing of the hospital—
otherwise known as *the basement.*
The first identical black quadruplets

rest peacefully all in a row.
The doctor has pumped their mother
full of vitamin C treatments. She
cannot read or write. The doctor

takes such burdens upon himself.
He negotiates the contract with
Pet in St. Louis. Staged beside
cans of their evaporated milk—

the God names thing one: *Mary Alice.*
the God names thing two: *Mary Ann.*
the God names thing three: *Mary Catherine.*
the God names thing four: *Mary Louise.*

The doctor makes the babies up.
He returns them to their tobacco farm,
sends them home to a glass-enclosed
nursery with viewing hours from two

until four. Their mother, deaf and mute,
eyes her angels through a finger-smudged
wall of glass. Her babies' bodies
propped up for observation.

She runs her finger along the placard
beside her girls' faces, her children
cataloged without permission.
She has six other mouths to feed.

Her husband, a sharecropper, has never
brought home more than $500 a year.
He calls his daughters small blessings
from heaven, says, *hail Mary, full of grace,*

the Lord is with thee over each
crib every night. They are his four
little stars, their first birthday on
the cover of *Ebony* magazine.

Child Witness

*I bring a little child that he might tell future
generations what is now agreed to.*

inscription above the South Carolina mural
Saluda Old Town Treaty, July 2, 1755

Call me little. I thread strands of
promise through his hair—

white as the tufts of a rabbit's back-
side as it hops across a landscape

of black. Leaves fall like men from
the sky. The muskets' noses rest

in the dirt like dogs' muzzles
sniffing in thick stalks of grass.

The white man's hand rests on
his thigh. He does not touch

the table my grandfather made
in the glow of yesteryear's thunder.

There is no happiness here, amongst
men that can weave lies out of light.

Old Hop holds a bow in one hand,
in his other hand an arrow of mercy.

The howls of my belly hang from
the holes of the sun's pierced ears.

I am small enough to keep time. I stand
guard. I stay still as threat comes close.

I watch for the faceless future,
which emerges bending down-

ward from the woods,
the past slung like a doe

across its shoulders, as history
repeats its hunger.

Lost Causes

In Paraguayan folklore there are seven monsters.
The Guarani say Kurupi comes at night,
his penis wound several times tight around
his waist, making a belted vestment.

His reach extends through the windows.
A scapegoat for how a woman could come
to be with child. How an eleven-year-old
gives birth after rape.

My mother is indigenous to nowhere. My lips curl in blood
at the rising of the father. Black is not a primary color.
A brown woman can still get killed for saying *no*.
How do hips learn to sound out a child?

On All Fours

A jaguar whips its cat-o'-nine-tails,
a symbol of self-flagellation,
its spotted back stained with welts,
sins branded deep in a golden coat.
Whiskers glisten with beer and spit.

Water No Get Enemy

for Berta Cáceres, assassinated March 2016,
La Esperanza, Honduras

I swam the field.
Her body everywhere—blue cornflowers.

A dam of rocks:
clattering at her feet, seashells
of bullets collected from her hair. I sing
the body hydroelectric, *if you wan to*
go wash, na water you go use, blue
and damned, standing at the bank
of the Gualcarque River, telling it to keep
her name out its mouth.

The men came in the night:
the coffin of a constellation
on their shoulders. Sky full of five-
pronged nails—dull and glimmering
at the same time. Trigger fingers
groped threat. Unruly eyes
mirrored dark hands soiled with
terror and riddled with history's teeth.
Yellow thumbnails smudged memory.

The men own even the rain:
even the wet body, found with head full
of black curls rippling like waves. No need
to roll the stone away; these women
don't rise on the third day, blinking
in the moonlight, wrapped in invisible
wire like something beautiful
is gonna come.

I sing the body hydroelectric:
if water kill your child, na water you go use.
Her flightless voice written on the sound
of water running, the sound of gunshots
pattering feet upstream. The blood
the last thing to come rushing, begging
to be taken back home. Flag hung.
The ribbon cut. Her lips aboard a ship,
the sky rocking her broken hips to sleep.
The shore—hard and unforgiving.

The field lies down before us.
The morning sun—a mistaken flame.

The Path of Totality

The front page of the *St. Louis Review* showed three nuns
staring up at the sky. The basic brown and white
of their habits in contrast to the gleam of eclipse glasses.
Sister Mary Francis stood in the middle. A pair of bifocals
dangled at her breasts. The callout to the left of her head
stated, *St. Louis embraced the total solar eclipse,
a fine example of God's grandeur.*

That day, I wrote a poem about God as the moon slipped
between the earth and the sun. The world went dim. I felt
nothing as my bare eyes silently burned, sight sacrificed in
my chasing after starlight. A blind poet takes up the pen
in the same way the sun eats fire. Self-destruction a form
of craft, an illustration of what a stanza can withstand.
All religion is art. Art is pain suffered and outlived.

Self-Portrait of Librarian with T.S. Eliot's Papers

In the year 2020, T.S. Eliot's papers will be unsealed.
Let us go then, you and I. Let us take the dust in
our claws, lap the hundreds of letters spilling secrets
into the wasteland of our irreverent mouths.
Have we no couth? Have we not been trained
to know good things come to those who wait?
Each year we gather round the cave. We don our Sun-
day best, come to see what young muse has risen
from the dead. Tomorrow brings the past wrapped
in plastic eggs, the seal of history broken in present tense.
Storage units preserve our culture's haunted houses.
The canon is merely a ghost story. Write a poem *after* me
before I'm gone, and please do not include *rest in peace;*
only those who are forgotten go undisturbed, only things
kept in the dark know the true weight of light.

To Whoever Is Reading Me

after Jorge Luis Borges

You are invulnerable.
The only thing constant is change.
Such repetition leads to nostalgia
for the present. Tense and timid
you recite this book by heart. Blind-
folded you commit me to memory.
The baldhead scallywag philosopher
knows that man's character is his fate.
This poem—not alive, but the remains
of a construct known as will.
Heraclitus is walking on water in Libya
or: *no man ever steps in the same river twice.*
Be wary of how the translator twists
my words, these ruins he interprets as
alive. Why do you dread being forgotten?
Know that in some sense
you are already dead.

All the World Began with a Yes

You don't say. Then a man takes
another man inside himself. Withdrawn,

his hands now rest in his lap. He counts out
the missing teeth and the varying stories

about how they came to be gone. The women
are displaced. Each an out-of-body experience.

I was beside myself, one remarks. A rib contradicts
its mirror image. Glass has mastered the art of

world building, the brevity of silence in self-
reflection. I am no authority on *what is out there,*

or the line between trespasser and trespassed.
Things without mouths cannot give consent,

but body language is a system of gestures.
The shoulders are experimental poets,

the legs offer no closure to sound.
The eyes dart, disturb the meter.

A relativity of rhyme or reason—was there ever
a time when I did not sell my body? I am ready

to turn in for the night. A full quiver.
Morality flexes its musculature, trusts

that truth sets out to penetrate mysteries,
only for man to rebuild them with fury.

The reality that this life is pleasurably
painful is something that I can rely on.

I had perceived you would leave. *I won't
not go,* you said. End: a burden of boon.

I don't know what it means *to hurt,*
on account of the signified signifier.

I am hungry and you are fearful.
The ocean is break-beat blue.

Desire: a longing damned.
A man once walked in on me

holding the mouth of a woman in
my own. *Live and let live,* an act of

grace, a folding of threat in on it-
self. Sorrow devours the image,

the hour of the star upon us.
So little has taken place.

II

The Library of Babel

for Jorge Luis Borges

While there is still some light
on the page, I am writing now
a history of snow, of everything
that has been and will be thought.
When a blind poet says *I need you
to be my eyes,* they are asking to see
through your mouth.

Free Radical

Before Gilgamesh invented
the kaleidoscope and Galileo
the Rubik's Cube, before the
scimitar-horned oryx went
missing, before the tamarind
trees went bare, before the
stars' eyelids were wrapped
in tinfoil, before the leaves
could gnaw on water, before
electrons made donations,
before the owl wore a mask,
before the wind had a sound,
before the moon had a name
and the smoke a spine, before
the tulips crossed their legs,
before the tongue was
armored, before the ghosts
rode centaurs to riots, before
cyberspace was culled and
belly buttons sewn to wombs,
before the taste had an after,
before intellect became
property and thunder
premeditated, before the
New, New World, before a
stone wished to be more
than a stone, before we had a
change of clothes, before the
grass was color-blind, before
the rivers lost their fingers
and the rain stopped teething,
before the kings were all
beheaded, their gravedigger
neither young nor old, before

a lion was still a lion, before
the girls were all killed, before
the trapeze gave way.   We
hung   suspended in time
by the arches of our curved
feet, and this tickled the gods,
tickled them to death.   And I
think our silence cut us loose,
let us go falling from the doubt,
secretly thrilled at the hems
and ever so eager to break.

The Librarian

I

She reads the *Atlas of World Languages in Danger
of Disappearing* while on lunch break. With turkey
sandwich in hand she types a note in her phone:
*Experts expect 90% of the world's approximately
7,000 languages will become extinct in the next 100 years.*
She thinks linguists build houses they can't afford
to finish. She thinks in theory, we will make it out
alive, the monsters under her bed are outdated,
they speak pidgin and bleed alphabet soup.
On her nightstand rests *A Street in Bronzeville*.
She plays word-search puzzles in neighborhoods
of vocabulary before the night lets down its hair.

II

The librarian is not the Spanish princess in *Pan's
Labyrinth*. She is Topsy from *Uncle Tom's Cabin*.
She spect she grow'd. She don't think nobody ever made her.
Autopsy comes from the Greek *autopsia* meaning:
a seeing for oneself. In her bed, when she makes love
she dissects the sounds, peels each syllable note
by note, deconstructs the prosody nailhead by
nailhead, until the clippings litter the omniscient
floor, already a basket—all the floorboards
hold pages of blank verse.

III

On Sundays sitting in coffee shops she wonders
if a computer can write a poem, if a machine has
consciousness. She finds the mouths of men stagnant,
sees men as horned beasts in their verbalizing.
Don't just talk about it, be about it, she contends.

She is from the Show Me State and people from
Missouri like to compromise. They bring slaves in
wicker baskets to picnics. The accompanying slices
of watermelon merely serve to suggest sincerity.

IV

Today the librarian learned that only humans can pick
up on sarcasm intuitively, that AI has yet to grasp
these finer nuances. The librarian lives in the gray,
she never mistakes what it looks like for what it is.
The Turing test serves as her bible. She has better things
to do than watch the eyes move of people who don't love her.
To love is to fear by choice, and fear is a particular religion.

Keep your day job, the professor had told her. *You could never
make a living as a poet.* But this is good work, she thought,
placing the black spines back in order, cupping
mouths of things that need to be shelved.
She believes every throat is a call number.
She puts each one back where it belongs:
808.02 C449T:E, 810.98 M882P, 814.54 L867S.
Her mother taught her you should never look
a gift horse in the mouth, so instead she feels
inside their covers. She was named without
her consent. *Pandora* means: *the girl with all the gifts.*

Ophiocordyceps unilateralis: the mind has a mind of its own: a black carpenter playing little red riding hood: a wolf waiting to hear footsteps in the forest: an unhealthy attachment to one's spouse: mistletoe is parasitic to trees: *hijack* another word for *bewitch:* it's around Christmas when your family begins to notice: something about you has changed: they can't quite put their finger on it: your face takes on a sacrificial tint: something different hidden just behind the eyes: the germ of malicious intent: perhaps it's the tic or the nail-biting: the habits you have suddenly picked up: your mental state as you lie prone on the floor: legs hot-wired by fungal puppeteer: hacking into your mainframe: trisected body a holy trinity: a temple occupied by a terrorist: the classification of the terror determines whether looting or foraging has taken place: the meaning of *ransacked* vs. *looked through:* the home a hollow shell of surrender: the suicide bomber takes organs hostage: the host attracts spectators to the scene: the mind is a terrible thing to waste and yet it never seems to do any good: it never gets over the matter: it takes on a life of its own: it eats you up inside to know this maxim: the bit in your mouth a death grip: the mace sticking out from back of your head: you adhere yourself to the wall of Plato's cave: transfixed by the shadows projected: the flames seem to snicker at the stake: the friendly fire—truth at its best:

The Code Talkers

I

Frost's "The Road Not Taken" is the most
misread poem in America   an example of
something everyone knows and yet gets
wrong   like *water is life* being a secret
code for why storms are given first names
the body a whodunit   a plot to be cracked
conspire from the Latin verb *spirare* meaning
to breathe with   man is closest to hurricane
the lungs holding him down until it's over

During the war, *TKOH* was the Navajo code word
for *water*   *water* translates to *aqua* in Latin
its gender feminine   the birthing place
or root word for *aquatic*   meaning
growing or living in water   meaning
wanting to *serve one's country*   meaning being
sent to boarding school   to learn
English—or the language the waves make
when they crash   the crest a jawbone afloat

The killing fields   a baptism   a desert boy praying
in a rain of fire   he had never seen the ocean
before enlisting as a Marine   never felt salt burn
ears ringing as shells plowed into the beach's
sandman fleet   the Navajo word for *convoy*
is *TKAL-KAH-O-NEL*
which translates to *moving on water*
following the Vulgar Latin *conviare* which means
literally "go together on the road"

He is not alone as he peeks out from the foxhole
red-eyed flashlights piercing the dark
see the bilingual Navajo (bloodshot on the outside

milk spill on the inside)   he unloads his rounds
eggshells the architecture of grief
the white noise a mare haunting his insomnia
a coyote sniffing the snow like glue
trying to cut or paste its way back home
a golden piss trail left in its wake

II

The tech world says   *coding is the new literacy*
programming tests that aim to *break your code*
meaning present it with some kind of input
that it is ill-equipped to handle thus making
your code blow up
                          or deliver results that are absurd
in other words put copper heads in
wet fatigues and see whether their faces turn green
think tanks built to make America great again

Growing up I worked summers at the St. Louis Zoo
its north entrance called The Living World
on display a lifelike mannequin of Lucy   a hairy
female with human hands and feet but apelike head
few visitors are aware that this is a misrepresentation
the fossil ape *Australopithecus afarensis* known to be
a long-armed knuckle-walker with locking wrists
my city was a planet of the apes to me back then
Lucy and I punching the time clock each morning

My junior year of Catholic high school I took
a service trip to a pueblo in New Mexico
taught English and math to children who lovingly
called me a Jemez word for *poop*   my being
the only black volunteer they had ever seen   I will
never forget my last day there   or the girl who
chased after our bus as we pulled off   the cotton

bolls of our eyes both displaced   dark irises pick-
pocketing their way through the window

April is National Poetry Month   and so I make
rounds at my hometown's inner-city public schools
I often hear them shouting, *the library lady is here!*
in the hallways   each one of my teeth the white
of a book page left out to yellow in the direct light
of the sun   all colors being subject to turning
        doubting that they should ever come back
two roads diverged in a wood less traveled
        a sheep in wolf's clothing is at the fork

Report from inside a White Whale

Biblioteca Vasconcelos in Mexico City
holds a massive, white whale skeleton.
I once climbed inside the belly on a visit.

I did it knowing that one day Cali will be
gone, the whole state swallowed by water,
my body a boat with holes, my limbs in need

of a ship. I found a man named Jonah in
the gullet taking field notes. I asked him
to serve as my witness. You should always

have someone to record—a historian,
a spouse, or a child will do just fine.
We made music in the bowels of that beast.

Jonah spit when he talked. We were Bone
Thugs-n-Harmony, joined at the cross-
roads of wildfire and revelry like knuckle-

heads of stone and skin. Our outer
limits flanked with a flood of the blues,
the archaeology of loss afloat.

I never once asked Jonah to cover his mouth,
but I believe I understood what he was saying:

*how dare the two of us make art when
god has ordered us to drown.*

Elephants Born without Tusks

The *Washington Post* says that green burials are on
the rise as baby boomers plan for their futures,

their graves marked with sprouting mushrooms,
little kneecaps crawling up from the dirt's skin

like Michael Brown decomposing into the concrete
ending as a natural product of the environment.

Elephants are now being born without tusks,
their genetics having studied the black market,

DNA a spiral ladder carefully carved
from wooden teeth of Founding Fathers.

Never let a chromosome speak for you, it will
only tell a myth—an ode to the survival of the fittest.

Peppered moths are used to teach natural selection,
their changes in color an instance of evolution.

Birds unable to see dark moths on soot-covered trees.
The number of blacks always rising with industry.

Life is the process of erosion, an inevitable wearing down
of the enamel. The gums posing the threat of disease.

Most websites suggest biodegradation,
a coffin made from pine or wicker.

The man in the paper said, *I want to be part of a tree,
be part of a flower—go back to being part of the Earth.*

I imagined my mother then, her short-cropped hair
like freshly cut grass, immune to the pains of mowing.

*The Natural Burial Guide for Turning Yourself into a
Forest* sits waiting in my Amazon shopping cart.

Pink salmon have now evolved to migrate earlier.
I am familiar with this type of Middle Passage,

a loved one watching you move on without a trace,
the living inheriting an ocean of time,

the sun rewiring the water-damaged insides,
cells desiring to go back where they came from,

certain strands of
your kind now extinct.

Portrait of a Pack Horse Librarian

The girl hears the snap
and crunch of hooves,
like the sound of rabbit
bones broken in the woods.
She stands in the doorway
barefoot. The library lady's
horse appears to be smoking
a pipe. Clouds of frost puff
from its wide nostrils. The girl's
mother greets the librarian, sees
the rain has soaked through
the librarian's shoes the way her
husband's tongue has stewed
all night in corn likker. Hunger thaws
in the girl's belly. The librarian combs
the growl's hair with a song. The girl's
chipped front tooth gleams dull against
the backdrop of the closing door's shadow.
There are countless stars in the pitch-
black sky, yet the girl still has so few
words. Now, she sits on the floor,
cradles a book like a toy boat in her lap.
Determined, the librarian rides farther
down the creek. She's learned a girl is
carved from the words she does not know.

Fiery Young Colored Girl

My grandmother had four children,
my father the first to be born.
She went to school alongside him
as the first colored secretary of Quincy
High. Monday through Friday she care-
fully applied her nude panty hose.
Every morning she listened to the sound-
track of her heels as she teetered down
the stairs to the school's basement.
Her role was to work out of sight from
the public, to file records by the glow of
one flickering lightbulb. She organized
the school's records for the state.
One day she let her red nails wander
and managed to stumble upon her own.
She cringed in the shadow of her frame
on the wall, studied the curves of her
teacher's perfect penmanship.
Beneath her name on her
final transcript:
fiery young colored girl
sensitive about race

A Valid Archive

000		01117cam a22002891 4500
001		2168301
005		20040616144635.0
008		800124s1965 nyuc j 000 0ceng
035	__	|9 (DLC) 65011811
906	__	|a 7 |b cbc |c orignew |d u |e ocip |f 19 |g y-gencatlg
010	__	|a 65011811
040	__	|a DLC |c DLC |d DLC
042	__	|a lcac
043	__	|a n-us---
050	00	|a PS153.N5 |b R6
082	00	|a [920] |2 19
100	1_	|a Rollins, Charlemae Hill.
245	10	|a Famous American Negro poets, |c by Charlemae Rollins.
260	__	|a New York, |b Dodd, Mead |c [1965]
300	__	|a 95 p. |b ports. |c 22 cm.
490	0_	|a Famous biographies for young people
520	__	|a Brief biographies of twelve African American poets with examples of their best-known works, from Jupiter Hammon of the eighteenth century to today's Arna Bontemps and Gwendolyn Brooks.
650	_0	|a African American poets |x Biography |x Juvenile literature.
650	_0	|a African Americans |x Intellectual life |x Juvenile literature.
650	_1	|a Poets, American.
650	_1	|a African Americans |x Biography.
991	__	|b c-GenColl |h PS153.N5 |i R6 |p 00018670513 |t Copy 1 |w BOOKS

Public Domain

You catalog by hand, playing librarian in your dead
mother's house. Try to justify archiving each item:

A balanced checkbook. Mothballs. Life Savers
mints. Back copies of the *New York Times.*

Frozen chicken potpies. The Yellow Pages.
Expired Lorna Doone cookies. Panty hose.

A pair of Daniel Green slippers from
Lord & Taylor. Flat Canada Dry ginger ale.

You find a little girl hiding in Mr. Rogers's mustard
sweater, sew on and sew forth, threading needles

with pubic hairs discovered in the carpet. Surreal
smells. The Pine-Sol dying down in the bathroom.

Which was your father's bad ear? The one that lost
most of its hearing in the war. There is life in the eyes

unspoken. Your very pulse a secret algorithm, a soft-
ware designed to track your browsing history.

An open casket on view for the whole church to see.
Her genetic code made available for live streaming.

You copyright the notes in the margins of her Bible.
The intellectual property preserved. Shaky cursive

her signature trademark. Upon the fall of a domestic
sphere, a pocketbook is emptied of all its valuables.

To become takes a long time. Blue spells are periods of
red where you pause, the body calculating the losses.

Library of Small Catastrophes

I

The pupil is a decimal point
surrounded by white matter.
The decimal place is a safe
house of absence. Place is
to home as story is to lie,
and every word is a cock
we teach to crow.

II

In the MFA class I have never had
the opportunity to take, they are dis-
cussing meter. In my mind, I struggle
to convert meters to feet.

The US is the only industrialized
country that does not use the metric
system. Beneath the desk, I use my
fingers to silently

count the decibels of distance, this
shame of being black and American.
As a woman, I am either stressed
or unstressed in theory.

Math is poetic in nature. You move
the decimal point two places to the right
to multiply black bodies
by the hundreds.

Voiceless. I am qualified to write wordless
poems. I use tongued commas, hangnail
earlobes, peacocks, diphthong asses that
don't sit well with readers.

III

I now have my MLIS. I've learned
the science to the system of classifying.

Repeat: *I know you are but what am I.*
Language in and of itself indoctrination.

Dear Dewey Decimal System,
How will I organize all the bodies?

The professor said that in judging
women's bodies by their covers

we have a system for returning
things back to where they belong.

IV

Once, while working the closing shift
in an Andrew Carnegie library,
I watched a woman get searched
for setting off the metal detectors.
I faced the officer's back, his shoulders
like the frame of a closed door.
He asked whether she had needles in
her pockets before he reached his
hand inside her pants.

The tip of a needle is the width
of a decimal point. A decimal is
the size of a pinprick. A finger
can resemble in look and feel
a penis.

The woman was taken down-
town, was booked for stealing
urban romance novels.
The ridges of her fingertips
filled with ink that bled.

In the nineteenth century for the first time
fingerprints were used to identify
repeat offenders. I can no longer
recall the woman's face, only
the beauty in the way her hands

trembled. She thought she had
removed the magnetic strips from her
person. She had done so in secret,
away from the cameras overhead.

In a bathroom stall, she broke
books' spines. She ripped their pages.
Her life a chapter of a book
she did not buy.

In my car I washed my hands of her,
the wave of terror that stained her face,
her pleas through the window of the cop's
backseat. The sound fell silent as the
open mouths of traffic lights.
The officer—green.
The woman, red bone
or high yellow, sits

slant in a cell. As she sleeps
with her head against the wall, the concrete
imprints braille into her face. She is a vampire,
each book a mirror she could not see her-
self in. Her insides dog-eared by syringes
that want to pick up where they left off.
Like me she had always liked to read in the dark.
Her mother had warned her, too. Said, *you need to
turn on a light, before your eyes go bad.*

And Then There Were None

White Teeth begins with
the epigraph, *What is past*
is prologue. The history of
the future as uncertain as
this gold crown. *Teeth hadst*
thou in thy head when thou
wast born, to signify thou camest
to bite the world, said King
Henry VI, the tenth little
nigger to die in the novelist's
vivid imagination. This is the
stuff that dreams are made of,
a man in a woman's bed, dead
to the world, dead as a door-
nail lodged inside a black boy's foot.
It was the thorn that said *good rid-*
dance to the boy, freedom a fore-
gone conclusion of pain. Stretch
marks tell a woman's backstory, and
story is to lie as boy is to man.

Oral Fixation

When I was born my father
was studying for the bar,
instead of sitting at one,
eyes glazed as they stared

at bourbon in glasses.
He was in labor when
he missed the wet pupils of my
eyes emerge, my mother unable

to get hold of him in time.
He taught me then what it
means to miss someone
you've never even met.

When I question the level
of dysfunction in my family,
my father likes to reason,
at least you don't

have an alcoholic for a parent.
This scale of evaluation
tragically soothes,
the way a sip of Southern

Comfort settles down into
the warmth of your chest.
Once, when my mother
had to work late,

my father, frantic and
helpless, allowed my
little lips to clamp onto his
nipple. He did not know

how else to keep me from crying.
My mother entered their bed-
room with her blouse soaked
under her suit. I wish I could

remember the way she looked
then, whether amused or dis-
gusted by my father's ability
to problem solve.

Even a baby knows the link be-
tween latch and leak.
My mother latched on harder
to my father while he took his

morning leak in the bathrooms
of other women's houses. He lost
his wedding band in the drain of a
hotel sink. The slippery slope

of cheap soap chafing to the skin.
He washed his dirty work down with
nice cologne. All husbands acquire
expensive taste. They empty them-

selves into a body of work,
produce children like islands cut off
from the mainland. Men want praise
for the strength of what they take in

their mouths, praise for not watering
down dark liquor with Coke. A husband
is a chaser. A wife is a woman of substance.
Substances can be used in different ways;

this depends on the laws of your love
language. The jury's still out on the ruling
state of sentiment: the domain of the heart,
mind, or body. The father of fickle palate

waits outside the pub near my apartment.
I scan the sea of backwash men, their torsos
flopping over like multiplying fish. Later,
when I am alone, I think of the ways

in which a parent can be there without being
physically present. Is it enough that my father
thinks of me often rather than choosing
to show his face? My social anxiety bites

his style, his need for absence, when I nurse
drinks in the heat of the empty night.
My lips suckle at the moon's dry breast.

Five and a Possible

Spades is a way of life for black folks.
My mother went into labor
In the middle of a game.
I was born as

Five and a possible. She said
She'd felt no greater pain than that loss,
Than when she turned away, shamefaced
In the midst of kin,

When certain bragging rights began to crown.
They pulled my body from her diamond,
Held me up to meet her gaze, to study
The odds of what a luckless god had

Given. An overbid could get you shot
At Grandma's house, could have you
Question the number of hearts
You had in your hand.

Everyone knew that my mother was the score-
Keeper. She counted the books twice every
Round. There had been three before me.
Babies my mother got but did not get.

My mother taught me to watch a man's eyes
When he deals, to cut the deck
Like his cord of wishful
Thinking.

She'd warn in silence, *don't talk across the table!*
Then demonstrate over dinner with my father,
As the air held the weight of
Things unsaid.

After the divorce and Grandma's funeral,
All the words in my mother for *tired*
Were tired, her hands folded
Like cards.

How Not to Remember

I don't remember that happening.
I mean I never did that. *Did you just*
make that up? says the mother to the daughter.
This whole family is imagined to begin with.
Let's try to make believe with our hands,
work the lies into a paste-like consistency,
coat the eyelids with the residue of denial.
Fabricated means cut from the same cloth
as your father. *Falsify:* calcified bones
in the belly of an impostor. In hard times
we rely on the promise of things to come.
Have your way with me, truth said in surrender.
Memory hastily unbuttoning soiled trousers.
I watched my stepmother empty the prayer beads
of a pomegranate into a Tupperware container
for my father. I was offered a few just to try.
To practice swallowing requests for god—
undressed of his leathery red skin.
I had heard they were good for liver health,
rich in antioxidants. They sometimes call them
jewels of winter. Funny how that summer my dad
developed cancer. My mother likes to tell the story
of how she ate a bratwurst right before I was born.
Aller Anfang ist schwer translates to *all beginnings are hard.*
When I was teething, she would glide her finger
against the inside of my mouth, rubbing my back
molars gently with oil of clove. She did this to
naturally make the aching stop. She does it now.
Again. This time with feeling.

III

born [again]

She sat in the abortion clinic in Virginia.
Her mother on guard from the mono-
chrome black-armed chair. The woman
appeared determined, as though she did
not question what she was capable of doing.
She looked older than she ever had before.
She no longer played on the moral seesaw
of right and wrong. He was the wrong man
to make a father, again. This was the wrong
time for her to be a mother. All the things
in the world depend on timing. The baby
would have only grown to hate her; it would
have inherited this cross from its father.
She could not hold such hatred to her breast
let alone find the strength to give it a name.
The unborn voice inside her said, *if you know
better, do better.* She responded with,
only a man can kill, only a woman can take a life.
On the drive home, she turned to her mother
and asked, *are you not born again when something
inside of you dies?* She waited months to receive
an answer. It didn't click until Mass, Ash
Wednesday, when Father told her, *you are dust,
and unto dust you shall return.* Her forehead smudged
with ashes black as midnight's back. Her face
trembled beneath his finger. *Parting is such sweet
sorrow,* said this woman who had done a thing
beyond the scope of mercy. This is what it
means to become: to do things you had never
imagined you would do, to be a furious flower—
murderous and innocent as water.

mer·cy *n*. **1a.** An act of divine favor or compassion; **b.** as in, 'twas *mercy* brought me from my Pagan land; **c.** 'twas grace soft as death at my mother's hands; **d.** a body on its way from one house to another. **2a.** A blessing; clemency; **b.** as in, saying politely, *I believe you have something of mine*; **c.** as in, what a mother whispers to a tree branch; **d.** as in, a razor blade that yields; **e.** the moon playing chicken with the sun. **3a.** A disposition to be kind and forgiving; **b.** as in, a prayer for sinners now and at the hour of death; **c.** as in, 'twas Jill playing jacks on the Hill; **d.** as in, mind over matter. **4a.** Something for which to be thankful; **b.** as in, a passing ship; **c.** a called game; **d.** enough food and a doorknob; **e.** a few teeth left. **5a.** Charitable treatment; **b.** as in, right before the fall; **c.** as in, ain't none of us truly free; **d.** we is all at the *mercy* of time.

Cento for Not Quite Love

and did i leave him or dream i left him?
"my husband,"
this man who said, "it is always better
than neutral, which is to say i'm sorry
to have to love you this way

took me   thirty years to say
i lost my own name in the shower
brief & miraculous, as the bees
bats, maybe, or owls, boxy mottled things

i married—years before i carried, within me,
sequins   sheet music   painkillers   any
birds, flowers, people, words.

                    * * *

if ever two were one, then surely we.
they call it sacrifice—   imagine me a tiny poppy
afraid of my clumsy body,
that impossible weight
the not quite love
but i stayed silent because you were smiling.
and because i'm never happy

you were a collection
of any shape against a window,
of the intentions
i only half believed at the time

say: i am a professor from the university of stupidity.
i think from this distance
the goldfish of my genius hates you.

* * *

i want to go in the back yard now
i bet there are forests out there
tell me, is pain the garden's only plan?
my face is covered in fruit flies.
too many bugs & i want a divorce.

:   i practice the work of worms
i am that woman knitted into place
i was accustomed to being sewn
with moon-caked madness

i've been pregnant. i've had sex with a man
who exposed the hairy, buff eggs
of a girl gazing at the moon.
there is a baby in my blood.
i love and yet am forced to seem to hate,
i can't stand myself.
& so my love is awkward & ill-timed

* * *

this is my gift.
being missed. the horses
dressed in hooks.   my body   is a gift
to climb in. i'd swim the sea
water waving forever
fresh as stars.

we don't just forget the words for love, we
soak teeth. we
try not trying for a while

i have been woman
as other creatures, that have eyes—
because i see. i am what i have seen.

we used to lie eye to eye, breathing together
close to the
nights, by the light of whatever would burn:
this is how it is with love.

cruelty comes easy for some. to withhold love
there too must be machines
say the heart is an ungodly machine.
shed the machine.

cherries hemorrhage in their bowl.
my own toothbrush.
my black wig on the chair. i never meant
it will hurt
like a clue
what is a home? a guarded space,
domestication

sit in me and ask me
where i have been and my body answers,
beneath that slow-setting sun

this lust is not heterosexual.
and this is not a confessional,
pressed like stubborn flowers

it's not a goodbye fuck
because no one knew
i break things.

       * * *

there is no homonym for disappearing, only
the last of this blood
the instance of our parting
nothing but
craggy skeletons of a winter

Viva Voce

Benjamin Franklin taps his foot inside my mouth.
The Junto meeting will begin any second now.
Each member will take a seat on a molar, their behinds
settling into the worn grooves. A Venus
flytrap of flatulence. They pass gas and fan the
stench with old almanacs. The smell is gaudy.

Silence Dogood takes daily *air baths,*
sitting nude in front of my opened lips. Out of
sight, out of mind, a drawbridge to a white man's
wonderland. The toothed mandible forms a skyline
of trees. Cleanliness is next to godliness. I like portly
poets best myself, around the size and stature of a
Pablo Neruda. An ode to mouthfuls of artichoke.

Light refracts off Franklin's spectacles,
and I in turn am illuminated for hours. The help
hollows out the cow udder for stuffing. The cork
unseals the wine's messy hole, reddened and stained
as the chin of a ghost with lockjaw. The haunt sucking
the meat from the collarbone of time, left wounded
in the house of a friend. The body is a club of mutual
improvement, where I am ranked no higher than a fool.

For You

for Chris

Hips full of awkwardness & angst,
my body swayed in your parent's dimly
lit basement. You manipulated my love
handles in the dark.

We begged the night to not let go of us.
We—trombones trembling, anthro-
pomorphizing beneath a creaky
wooden staircase.

Cockeyed philosophical beasts,
we played bagpipes in the musty
air of Saturday nights. Albums
at our feet littered the floor

like flattened Imo's pizza boxes.
You gingerly twisted your curls
around your fingers, our cosmic eye-
lids heavy as sandbags before a flood.

This was all before, before you took
your life in the U. City park pond,
your bloated body pulled from
the algae-covered water,

before the day I sat on the yellow
couch in your living room, in my hands
a police-made photocopy of the suicide
letter you had left for me.

The original still sits in a file at some
precinct, further evidence of the distance
between us. I wonder, is the drawer
ever left ajar, a gray mouth

that hangs open as if to say, *please go on.*
We have forsaken the sacredness of sound,
the precise quality of a loved one
saying your name aloud.

I can't remember the last time I heard
your voice, your last voicemail trapped
on an obsolete cellphone, the battery
dead and charger nowhere to be found.

I can still see your mother from my seat
on the sofa, the way her body bent
in pleas, lips quivering as they howled,
a mother should never have to bury her child.

I abandoned your house and my home-
town. Ran from your body caught on
record, dipped from the feel of lips
I could no longer put my finger on.

The loss of your smell, a trail of guilt
that led me every day to the doorstep
of want. I have been meaning to stop
by your mom's, to stand awhile

at the edge of that pond in the park,
to at least swing by your resting place
with microphone-shaped flowers—
hyacinths the color of purple rain.

The Beastangel

after Robert Hayden's "Bone-Flower Elegy"

In the dream I enter him
I   the eater of numbers
the black-lipped bar code
of cost have come for him
because he owes me. He
owes me the broken machine
the bone structure gone limp
over leg of time. I   irreverent
as safe sex breathlessly
whispering *this is not a threat*
but a promise for the love of
the wolf on lockdown. *Why*
the long face? the horsefly
asked the muzzle as though to
suggest these mouths we
have are traps   boldfaced lairs
of brotherhood. Cover your eyes
and you'll miss it   you'll miss this
squalid city growing legs from its
scalp. His kneecaps jerked beneath
the sheet   skinned eyelids rolling back
to the   *Point to where he touched*
you on the doll   he asked.
¿Cómo se dice "everywhere"?
He will pay for this   the heroic
antihero announced   the vulture-
masked man surveying the damage
the clinical centaur now spooked
reared up as if to say
demons fear beasts in twos.
Rage bound tight in synthetic
skin   bound and ridden in dialect

at an angle of consumption. After
feeding he asks   *what's the damage?*
The legless caterpillar humping itself
forward   toward my mouth   rending
the lip   a cleft palate   twisted up from
firegold sand   a habit of creature
malformed. The men lay flowers
on my mother's tongue   they come
see about me. These flowers are edible
men   flowers of sawtooth bone.

A Rock Trying to Stand

after photograph bearing caption "The body of Big Foot, a chief of the Miniconjou Sioux, lies frozen in the snow that covered the bloody battlefield at Wounded Knee on December 29, 1890"

It has never been proved that heat rises
that copper burns green when set on fire.

Spotted Elk's head tilts back at the eagle-bone whistle
sound jumping from the hill of Wounded Knee.

The squeal earmarks the edge of the South Dakota sky
sullen winds having looked right through the body.

Tongue—the spoon the ancestors hold
ladling the Great Spirit's song as spittle

drops spilling through
the ivory teeth of clouds.

Remember the time the salmon committed suicide
their shiny eyes glowing slivers of silver in the dark?

Somewhere a man weeps glass
in his blue Chevy pickup

visions forecast on a dirty windshield
sky splayed with exploded two-winged stars.

It's a lie to think the rain is not hungry
the creek water flooding lickety-split

coming to lick the spaces between our toes
each crevice starved for crumbs of light.

The living rocks still talk in their sleep
supple secrets stored in cracks of eyelids.

Yesterday we walked to where the river runs
sideways like a twisting snake lost in its skin.

I felt a wild dog's femur bone succumb underfoot
the way the hours bark at the moon to come home.

There is no word for "nature" in Onondaga
no distance between the life support and life.

What is the chemical composition of a verb vs. a noun
the dissonance between a coyote's laugh and cough?

I have watched an ant nibble at the sun's arm
having prayed beforehand—to avoid catching fire.

The brother I never had joined the circle of dancing
the neck of his beer grown warm on the truck hood.

Legend has it when the men first started to ghost dance
they numbered only a hundred or so.

But they were twice that number by the end
no one new having entered the ring.

That summer the buckwheat had shone like fox fur
the whiskered dead having arrived to take up alms.

A body falls like grass before the sickle.
See the limbs frozen like a stone stick figure's

the toy Indian's arms and legs contorted
ball-and-socket joints all askew.

An action figure abandoned in the plains
winter's sticky fingers soon cropping up.

Icicles ornament each note of stillness
like feathers dripping loss from thin air.

White sage embraces the nostrils' ovals
the way life unfolds in a circle.

A bullet drums now in Big Foot's head.
A red man is dancing in the snow.

Why Is We Americans

We is gator teeth hanging from the rear-
view mirror as sickle cells suckle at Big
Momma's teats. We is dragonfly
choppers hovering above Walden Pond.
We is spinal cords shedding like the skin
of a cottonmouth. We is Psalm 23 and
the pastor's chattering chicklets. We is
a good problem to have. We is throats
constricting and the grape juice
of Jesus. We is Roach and Mingus in
Birdland. We is *body electric,* eyes
watering with moonshine, glossy lips
sticky with lard. We is half brothers in
headlock, arm wrestling in the dirt.
We is Vaseline rubbed into knocked
knees and cracked elbows. We is ham
hocks making love to kidney beans. We
is Orpheus, lyre in hand, asking *do we
have a problem?* We is the backstory
of myth. We is sitting horse and crazy
bull. We is brown paper bags,
gurgled belches. We is hooded ghosts
and holy shadows roaming Mississippi
goddamned. We is downbeats and
syncopation's cousin. We is mouths
washed out with the blood of the lamb.
We is witch hazel–coated backs sucking
on peppermint wrappers. We is the
spiked antennae of a triangle-faced
praying mantis. We is barefoot
tongue-tied hogs with slit throats and
twitching bellies. We is sun tea and
brewed bitches. We is the crying
pussies that stand down when told to

man up. We is Radio Raheem and Zoot
Suit Malcolm. We is spit-slick low cuts
and fades. We is scrappy black-masked
coons and turkey-necked bullfrogs. We
is the pits of arms at stake, the clouds
frothing at the mouth. We is swimmers
naked, private parts Whitman allegedly
fondled beneath the water. We is
late lurkers and castrated tree limbs
on the Sunday before last. We is red-
veined pupils and piss-stained knickers,
slack-jawed and slumped in the
bathroom doorway. We is whiplash
and backhanded ways of settling grief.
We is clubbin' woolly mammoths
upside the head, jammin' fingers in
Darwin's white beard. We is comin'
round yonder, pigeon-toed and
bowlegged, laughin' our heads off.
We is lassoed cowboys swingin' in
the sweet summer breeze.

Manifesto, or Ars Poetica #3

after Luciano Concheiro

Start with a common enemy. Time.
What do we hate most? The present.
And even more than that? History.
In the future, poetry is dead.
We spend more time dead than alive.

Word of Mouth

after a Nick Cave Soundsuit made from buttons
and a found vintage abacus

When George Washington became president in
1789 he had only one tooth in his head, a single
premolar poking up from his gums. His dentures
were fashioned from lead, gold wire springs,
brass screws, the teeth of humans and cows,
elephant ivory, and hippopotamus bone. It is
a myth that he had false teeth made of wood.
A misperception put forth by those misled by
the hairline fractures that ivory and bone possess.
Just as cherry wine will stain cloth with a rust-hued vein,
Washington's beloved dark wine blemished
his teeth. The fractures eventually darkening, until
resembling the grain in a piece of wood.
The darkening of fractures is rather curious.
The makeup of the flesh, the constitution of
origin, the trackers of bloodlines thrown off the trail.
It is difficult to determine what discolorations
have tunneled their way through the body.
Spider veins climbing the back of my legs like a
river mapping trauma. An unspoken collective
of ephemeral bits and bytes, suffering
most eloquently preserved in the mouth. The skin
of one's teeth decides many a fate. A black woman's
incisor settling down inside a white man's maw.
Overall, a quizzical look, an off-color joke about
progress, the very blood a trick of the eye, an ocean-
blue on the outside of the skin, a blushing
red if viewed just beneath the sheath.

A tooth is made up of the crown and the root,
all the king's men destined to revolt. There are
many ways to worm your way inside, many open-

ings in the body of an animal. Some orifices gated
with white entryways. A wooden portcullis, a pick-
et fence, a laced corset secured tightly by a maid,
a pointed geode just waiting to be pulled, the cavern
wall glittering in the dark. Sharp crystals ornament
the cave's jawbone. *Cave canem,* quite naturally speak-
ing. A hooded hole a place for some to hide or go
seek. A toothless whistle the signal for the slave-
hunting bloodhounds, with canines fanged like
water moccasins'. The swamp mud gushing like
the suppertime mush sloshing between the gums
of a Confederate soldier. The terror of limbs at
odds with the self. In World War I, trench foot
meant frequent amputations, the blade sliding
like floss between the toes. Some diseases attack
the foot or mouth, with gums left inflamed in the
crossfire. A grieving mother wears dog tags
around her neck. Her son's baby shoes and teeth
cast in bronze. The pulp at the center is how the
tooth receives nourishment, how it transmits
signals to the brain. The forgetting makes the
present tense possible. Memory is the gravity
of the mind. All the icebergs have started to
melt, milky objects left hanging by a
string, the doorknobs' means to an end.

The keyboard's toothy smile splayed wide,
the flatlined cursor blinks impatiently on the
screen, my fingers struggle to tap into word
processing. I monitor all of the tracked changes.
Even the computer is a slave to death. Its in-
nards already bygone, its body obsolete upon
year of purchase. I am a librarian, swimming the
digital divide—my predecessor's paddles
a mass of floppy disks in an office closet.
They pile up like the teeth of slaves waiting

for sale. An affluent businessman at the closet door,
his hands panning the saliva for white gold.
His fingers parting the cavity, pursed lips cooing,
I need something of yours to call my own. The desire
to chew and smile at will. My grandmother lost
her mind before her teeth, lost the memories be-
fore the enamel gave way to rot. My face has my
mother's abacus features. We are in fact diphy-
odont. In one lifetime we develop two sets of teeth.
The missing space filled with air, a hollow exile
before the native tongue. I pray my unborn child
will have a gap. What the French call *dents du
bonheur* or lucky teeth. The womb's peephole is
rather impressionable. I will fasten the buttons of
time. I will take the baby's body in my own,
whisper a plea in its discriminating ear:
Try to keep your wits about you, my love.
Memory is about the future, not the past.

Overkill

Caesar wrote books by
the light of books burning

memory is an art form
forgetting is a science

poems are the living dead
the Bean Eaters never die,

nor does   "Lady Lazarus"
they're   *a sort of walking miracle*

the digital age shapes the future's
head   a stillborn screen

the pixel dilated   10 cm
the definition of a higher power

power   power to da lord
sinnerman, where you gonna run to?

the only thing constant is change
change   a metaphor for god

on the other side of god a death
on the other side of death a song

i hope   that you're the one
if not   you are the prototype

fetuses dance in formaldehyde
perfection cannot have offspring

a slippery slope of identity
the ship of Theseus puzzle

e-mail from Birmingham jail
a declaration of independence

bees' wings replaced w/ windmills
dogs' tongues replaced w/ Tasers

the rabbit neck snapped
the meat cured with salt

my water broke   in the night
i was just starting to eat for two

language never dies in my mouth
it plays dead at the foot of a cross

they are starting to call me brave
brave   a substitute for poet

What Is Tragedy?

Inside everything I have ever written
there is a girl—strange and alive.
Her sex is formed one image at a time:
pistachio shells in trash can, an animal
pretending to be dead, a fur-covered
moth, taffeta arranged in velvet clumps.
I know not what this world will do to
her or how her mother will someday
find her body. She sees white before
she blacks out, the texture of her
tongue like silt. If I slept with the girl
what would *sleep* imply? I stroke her hair.
Almost like a mother. I smell her as she
dreams of cottonwoods and caterpillars.
The light shifts and I am left childless
staring at the shape of fog. Someday,
when I am gone, this will all make sense,
how the girl held my poems like fetishes
in her mouth, sucked on words: *welt, sift,*
cleave, and *burr,* how poetic she was when full,
waiting quietly for terror to find her.

Object Permanence

For the time being
an ampersand is a boy
clutching his knees
to his chest as art.

On high, the god of form
wears a face on each wrist.
Only a god can take and give
time, *but the one in front of*
the gun lasts forever.

The boy is parenthesis,
his shoulders curved,
the huddled wings of a bird.

The boy's arms are too short
to box with god. He breaks down-
beats of sweat in his sleep.

If life is music, the rest is noise,
this earth a museum of dead boys
walking. The god has a finger to
his lips. He wakes to the boy

taking selfies with *The Scream*.
The boy knows a picture
will only last longer.

Frequent warnings read
Storage almost full across his
screen so self-portraits he
outsources to the cloud.

As I Lay Dying sits in his book
bag. The page dog-eared with
the sentence: *My mother is a fish.*

Right now
the comma
is a lobe.

From afar the god clutches
his head, in an effort
to cover missing ears.

The redbone boy was airborne.
As we speak, he bleeds in the street.
The backpack has landed as parachute.

The god yowls watercolors,
the way the sky weeps
oranges in lung-shaped
segments of grief:
quarter, half, a whole.

A bullet is a form of punctuation.
From a distance it appears
the boy is fucking up commas.
Roger that.

The god of variables—a-
bridged & for-
lorn—dribbles mercy
on the mother of
the slain.

The boy's headphones skip
down the sidewalk in the hands
of another mother's child.

The skeletal god's got bars.
A rib cage full of tally marks

collection plates in memory
of chicken-scratched bones.

The writing on god's wall
is formerly known as art.

* * *

The boy's chest has become
a focal point. It rests in
his mother's arms, a still-life painting.
The god is MIA.

The boy's mother repeats her prayers
again, & again, & again, & again, & again.

Repetition leads to the longing for a god,
for a sound as signal, for the absence of a note
or limb. Think of the bo(d)y as con artist.

The boy's mother knows a period is
something missed. She knows objects
can disappear behind a god's back
but that doesn't mean they are gone.

She holds the boy's cracked
phone in her hands, as if it were
the whole world.

A boy is what he leaves behind.
What a mother struggles to forget
her muscles store as memory.

Notes

"Skinning Ghosts Alive" borrows from Sylvia Plath's "Lady Lazarus" in *Ariel* and Vivek Shraya's *She of the Mountains*.

"mis·ery" makes reference to Thomas Jefferson's *Notes on the State of Virginia*. "mis·ery" and "mer·cy" borrow the form of A. Van Jordan's "in·cho·ate" in *M-A-C-N-O-L-I-A*.

"The Fultz Quadruplets" references the May 1947 *Ebony* magazine cover featuring a color photograph of the Fultz babies with the heading QUADRUPLETS' FIRST BIRTHDAY; the epigraph is from Tyree Daye's poem "Neuse River" in *River Hymns*.

"Child Witness" mentions Old Hop, whose Cherokee name is rendered as Connecorte or Kanagatucko.

"Water No Get Enemy" is the title of a Fela Kuti song on the album *Expensive Shit;* the poem features lines borrowed from Carl Phillips's "In Which to Wonder Flew a Kind of Reckoning" and "Since You Ask" in *Reconnaissance*.

"The Path of Totality" borrows a line from Robert Hayden's "The Tattooed Man" in the poetry collection *American Journal*.

"All the World Began with a Yes" takes its title from the opening line of Clarice Lispector's novel *The Hour of the Star*.

"The Library of Babel" features lines from Ilya Kaminsky's "Musica Humana" in *Dancing in Odessa*.

"The Librarian" features the call numbers for Hélène Cixous's *Three Steps on the Ladder of Writing*, Toni Morrison's *Playing in the Dark: Whiteness and the Literary Imagination*, and Audre Lorde's *Sister Outsider*.

"*Ophiocordyceps unilateralis*" borrows the form of Roger Reeves's "*Cymothoa exigua*" in *King Me*.

"The Code Talkers" features words from the *Navajo Code Talkers' Dictionary*, as found in Chester Nez's memoir *Code Talker*.

"Elephants Born without Tusks" refers to the *Washington Post* article "'Green burials' are on the rise as baby boomers plan for their future, and funerals," by Ellen McCarthy, October 6, 2014.

"Portrait of a Pack Horse Librarian" features research from Kathi Appelt and Jeanne Cannella Schmitzer's *Down Cut Shin Creek: The Pack Horse Librarians of Kentucky*.

"Fiery Young Colored Girl" is dedicated to my paternal grandmother, Betty Rollins.

"A Valid Archive" borrows the form of the Library of Congress Machine-Readable Cataloging (MARC) tags for librarian Charlemae Hill Rollins's book *Famous American Negro Poets.*

"Public Domain" is dedicated to my maternal grandmother, Dorothy Jackson.

"And Then There Were None" takes its title from Agatha Christie's mystery novel, which was first published in the UK as *Ten Little Niggers,* with American reprints and adaptations titled *And Then There Were None* after the last five words in the nursery rhyme "Ten Little Indians."

"Five and a Possible" borrows a line from Gwendolyn Brooks's "the mother" in *Selected Poems.*

"born [again]" drew inspiration from Sharon Olds's "I Go Back to May 1937" in *The Gold Cell.*

"mer·cy" makes reference to Phillis Wheatley's poem "On Being Brought from Africa to America." "mer·cy" and "mis·ery" borrow the form of A. Van Jordan's "in·cho·ate" in M-A-C-N-O-L-I-A.

"Cento for Not Quite Love" is composed entirely of lines borrowed (in their original form with changes only made to capitalization) from the following poets, in order of appearance: Diane Seuss, Ellen Bryant Voigt, Naomi Shihab Nye, Erika Meitner, Vievee Francis, Tiana Clark, Jacqui Germain, Aracelis Girmay, Natalie Diaz, Sharon Olds, t'ai freedom ford, Gigi Marks, Anne Bradstreet, Rebecca Hazelton, Diane Wakoski, Jessica Jopp, Yrsa Daley-Ward, Robin Coste Lewis, Lee Ann Roripaugh, Cathy Linh Che, Phillis Levin, Rachel Eliza Griffiths, Elizabeth Arnold, Marilyn Chin, Jorie Graham, Julie Sheehan, Gwendolyn Brooks, Akilah Oliver, Andrea Scarpino, Morgan Parker, Fatimah Asghar, Solmaz Sharif, Tracy K. Smith, CM Burroughs, M. NourbeSe Philip, Nicole Sealey, C.D. Wright, Rita Dove, Nayyirah Waheed, Queen Elizabeth I, Brenda Shaughnessy, Yona Harvey, Angel Nafis, Marty McConnell, Erika L. Sánchez, Safiya Sinclair, Lucille Clifton, Kiki Petrosino, Keetje Kuipers, Joan Murray, Elva Williams, Audre Lorde, Emily Dickinson, Janice N. Harrington, Freya Manfred, Eileen Myles, Eleanor Wilner, Joyce Sidman, Khadijah Queen, Jane Hirshfield, Traci Brimhall, Dawn Lundy Martin, Melissa Stein, Glenna Luschei, Lynda Hull, Sandra Simonds, Heather Phillipson, Sarah C. Woolsey, Tonya M. Foster, Tina Chang, Amber Flora Thomas, Jonterri Gadson, Sara Littlecrow-Russell, Ai, Sierra DeMulder, Evie Shockley, Anna Journey, Sandra Cisneros, Aricka Foreman, Naomi Ayala, Alice Walker, Elizabeth Bishop, and Lyrae Van Clief-Stefanon.

"For You" takes its title from the Prince album *For You* and is written in memory of Christopher Kevin Cahill (1986–2005).

"Why Is We Americans" borrows its title from Amiri Baraka.

"Manifesto, or Ars Poetica #3" mimics the title of Krista Franklin's "Manifesto, or Ars Poetica #2," published in *Poetry*, April 2015, and contains lines borrowed from Luciano Concheiro's *A Theory of the Manifesto or a Manifesto for Manifestos* as well as from the 1960 film *Macario*.

"Word of Mouth" refers to "George Washington Didn't Have Wooden Teeth—They Were Ivory," by Colin Schultz, Smithsonian.com, November 7, 2014.

"Overkill" takes lines from Nina Simone's song "Sinnerman" on the album *Pastel Blues* and OutKast's song "Prototype" on the album *Speakerboxxx/The Love Below.*

"What Is Tragedy?" borrows sentences from Lidia Yuknavitch's novel *The Small Backs of Children.*

"Object Permanence" features a line borrowed from Kendrick Lamar's song "Money Trees" on the album *Good Kid, M.A.A.D City* and Future's song "F*ck Up Some Commas" on the album *DS2.*

Acknowledgments

Thank you to the editors of the journals in which many of the poems in this book appeared, often in earlier forms:

ALIVE Magazine: "All the World Began with a Yes"

The American Poetry Review: "Elephants Born without Tusks," "Self-Portrait of Librarian with T.S. Eliot's Papers," "To Whoever Is Reading Me"

Crazyhorse: "How Not to Remember"

Hayden's Ferry Review: "The Code Talkers"

Indiana Review: "mer·cy," "Report from inside a White Whale"

New England Review: "Five and a Possible"

Poetry: "The Beastangel," "Free Radical," Object Permanence," "original [sin]," "Why Is We Americans," "Word of Mouth"

The Poetry Review: "Why Is We Americans"

River Styx: "Water No Get Enemy"

TriQuarterly: "Public Domain," "A Rock Trying to Stand"

Tupelo Quarterly: "Skinning Ghosts Alive"

Vinyl: "A Woman of Means"

"The Beastangel" and "Why Is We Americans" were also published in the anthology *Misrepresented People* (NYQ Books).

"Elephants Born without Tusks" also appeared in *ALIVE Magazine* online.

Many Thanks...

I offer endless thanks to my informal teachers, friends, and muses. I extend the deepest of gratitude to Phillip B. Williams for his genius insights, keen editorial eye, and never-ending encouragement. Many thanks to Justin Phillip Reed for having the vision and dedication to create his St. Louis–based Most Folks workshops where I twice had the pleasure of being a participant.

I send special light, love, and the audacity of hope to all librarian/artists, misfits, outcasts, and persons on the margins—keep writing, pushing, and believing. I see you.

For the gifts of craft, time, and financial support, I would especially like to thank Toi Derricotte, Cornelius Eady, and Nicole Sealey at Cave Canem; Greg Pardlo at the Callaloo Creative Writing Workshop; Monifah Lemons and Candace Wiley at The Watering Hole; the Rona Jaffe Foundation; the Bread Loaf Writers' Conference; and Don Share for the Poetry Foundation's Ruth Lilly Poetry Fellowship.

To Michael Wiegers and all the good folks at Copper Canyon, thank you for being champions of my dream.

For the memories of particularly lovely readings in my hometown of St. Louis, I thank the Pulitzer Arts Foundation, *River Styx*, and the St. Louis Poetry Center.

In closing, I thank my family: Grandma Dot for your strong will and front hallway lined with books; Grandpa Ted for your large hands and heart; Grandma Betty and Grandpa Luther for your vision and sacrifices; my mother, Susan, for filling my childhood with the sound of Roald Dahl's *The BFG* and for frequently taking us to the public library; my father, Luther, for trips to bookstores where you purchased countless books and music as an act of extending your values of education and literacy into our lives; and lastly my two sisters, Chandler and Ava, who I unequivocally adore and am lucky beyond measure to walk this earth alongside.

About the Author

Alison C. Rollins was born and raised in St. Louis City. Her poems have appeared in *The American Poetry Review, New England Review, Poetry,* and elsewhere. She is a 2016 recipient of the Poetry Foundation's Ruth Lilly and Dorothy Sargent Rosenberg fellowship and a 2018 recipient of the Rona Jaffe Foundation Writers' Award. She has also been awarded support from the Cave Canem Foundation, Callaloo Creative Writing Workshop, and Bread Loaf Writers' Conference. She holds a BS from Howard University and an MLIS from the University of Illinois at Urbana-Champaign. She has worked for the District of Columbia Public Library and St. Louis Public Library. Currently she works as a librarian at the School of the Art Institute of Chicago.

You can find her at www.alisoncrollins.com.

Poetry is vital to language and living. Since 1972, Copper Canyon Press has published extraordinary poetry from around the world to engage the imaginations and intellects of readers, writers, booksellers, librarians, teachers, students, and donors.

WE ARE GRATEFUL FOR THE MAJOR SUPPORT PROVIDED BY:

THE PAUL G. ALLEN
FAMILY FOUNDATION

TO LEARN MORE ABOUT UNDERWRITING
COPPER CANYON PRESS TITLES,
PLEASE CALL 360-385-4925 EXT. 103

WE ARE GRATEFUL FOR THE MAJOR SUPPORT PROVIDED BY:

Anonymous (3)

Jill Baker and Jeffrey Bishop

Anne and Geoffrey Barker

Donna and Matt Bellew

John Branch

Diana Broze

The Beatrice R. and Joseph A.
Coleman Foundation, Inc.

Laurie and Oskar Eustis

Mimi Gardner Gates

Nancy Gifford

Gull Industries, Inc. on behalf of
William True

The Trust of Warren A. Gummow

Petunia Charitable Fund and
advisor Elizabeth Hebert

Bruce Kahn

Phil Kovacevich and Eric Wechsler

Lakeside Industries, Inc. on behalf
of Jeanne Marie Lee

Maureen Lee and Mark Busto

Rhoady Lee and Alan Gartenhaus

Peter Lewis

Ellie Mathews and Carl Youngmann
as The North Press

Hank Meijer

Gregg Orr

Gay Phinny

Suzie Rapp and Mark Hamilton

Emily and Dan Raymond

Jill and Bill Ruckelshaus

Kim and Jeff Seely

Richard Swank

Dan Waggoner

Barbara and Charles Wright

Caleb Young as C. Young Creative

The dedicated interns and
faithful volunteers of
Copper Canyon Press

The Chinese character for poetry is made up of two parts:
"word" and "temple." It also serves as pressmark for
Copper Canyon Press.

The poems are set in Sabon.
Book design and composition by Phil Kovacevich.